KIDZBOP

COLLECTION OF POP HITS FOR YOUNG VOICES

Arrangements by TOM ANDERSON

TABLE OF CONTENTS

HAL•LEONARD®
CORPORATION

7777 W. BLUEMOUND RD. P.O. BOX 13819 MILWAUKEE, WI 53213

Visit Hal Leonard online at
www.halleonard.com

Best Day of My Life

Words and Music by
ZACHARY BARNETT, JAMES ADAM SHELLEY,
MATTHEW SANCHEZ, DAVID RUBLIN,
SHEP GOODMAN and AARON ACCETTA
Arranged by TOM ANDERSON

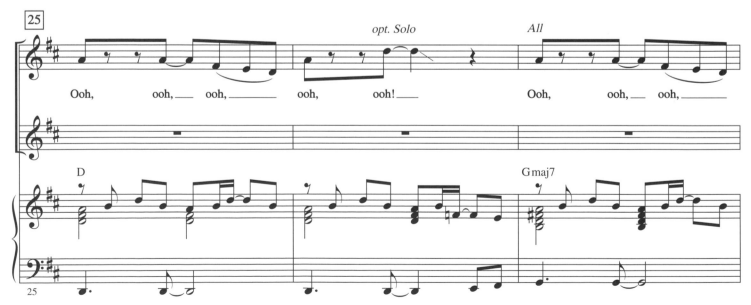

nev-er gon-na look back,___ whoa.___ I'm nev-er gon-na give it up,_____ no.___

Bm7   D

Just don't wake me now.___   This is gon-na be the best day of my

opt. Solo *f*

Ooh, ooh,___ooh,___ ooh.

G2   N.C.   D

All

life,___   my life.___

Ooh, ooh,___ ooh,___ my life.___   Ooh, ooh,___ ooh,

Gmaj7   D

Originally Recorded by RACHEL PLATTEN

Fight Song

Words and Music by
RACHEL PLATTEN and DAVE BASSETT
Arranged by TOM ANDERSON

lieves._____ 'cause I've still got a lot of fight left in me,_____

Huh!   Huh!

Em   D   C   N.C.   Em

46

_____ a lot of fight left in me._____ Like a small boat_

C   G   D   N.C.

49

[53]

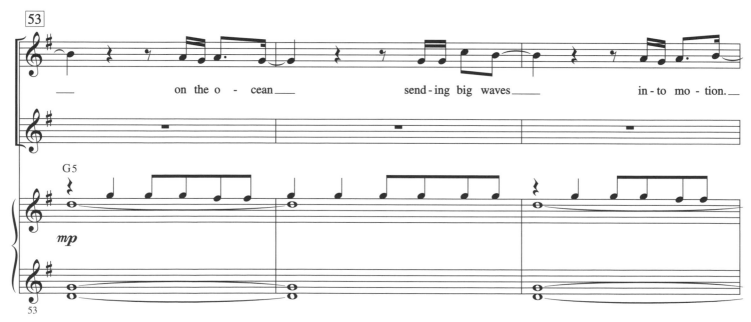

_____ on the o - cean_____ send - ing big waves_____ in - to mo - tion._

G5

mp

53

16

Roar

Words and Music by
KATY PERRY, LUKASZ GOTTWALD,
MAX MARTIN, BONNIE McKEE,
and HENRY WALTER
Arranged by TOM ANDERSON

28

Shake It Off

Words and Music by
TAYLOR SWIFT,
MAX MARTIN and SHELLBACK
Arranged by TOM ANDERSON

mm. But I keep cruis - ing; can't stop, won't stop groov - ing. It's

But I keep cruis - ing; can't stop, won't stop groov - ing. It's

like I got this mu - sic in my mind say-ing, "It's gon-na be al - right." —

like I got this mu - sic

hand claps

— 'Cause the play - ers gon - na play, play, play, play, play — and the

34

I'm just gon - na shake it 'til the fel - la o - ver there with the real - ly good hair, won't you

108

dance on o - ver, ba - by? We can shake, shake, shake.

Melody

opt. Harmony

'Cause the

ad lib. Solo

f

Yeah, _____ oh, _____

f

111

shake it off, I shake it off. I, I, I shake it off, I shake it off. I, I, I

ah.

end ad lib. Solo

Am7   C   G

hand claps

shake it off, I shake it off. I, I, I shake it off, I shake it off!

Oo,___ oo,   oo!

N.C.

Originally Recorded by MARK BRONSON
Featuring BRUNO MARS

Uptown Funk

Words and Music by MARK BRONSON, BRUNO MARS,
PHILIP LAWRENCE, JEFF BHASKER, DEVON GALLASPY,
NICHOLAUS WILLIAMS, LONNIE SIMMONS, RONNIE WILSON,
CHARLES WILSON, RUDOLPH TAYLOR and ROBERT WILSON
Arranged by TOM ANDERSON

good girls,___ straight mas-ter-piec-es. Styl-in', while in liv-in' it up___ in the cit-y. Got

Chucks on___ with Saint Lau-rent,___ got-ta kiss my-self, I'm so pret-ty. I'm too hot. (Hot, yeah!) Called the

po-lice___ and a fi-re-man. I'm too hot. (Hot, yeah!) Make a drag-on want___ to re-ti-re, man.___ I'm too

hot. (Hot, yeah!) Say my name,___ you know who I am.___ I'm too hot. (Hot, yeah!) Am I

43

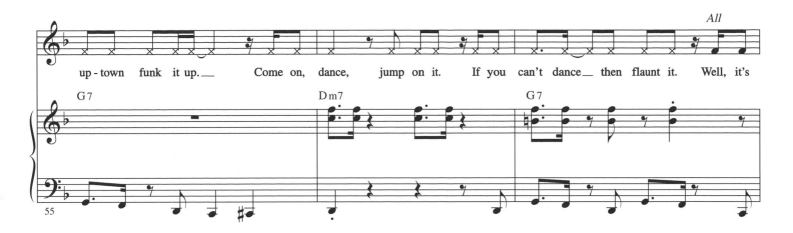

up - town funk it up.__ Come on, dance, jump on it. If you can't dance__ then flaunt it. Well, it's

Sat - ur - day night__ and we in the spot.__ Don't be - lieve__ me? Just watch. Come on!

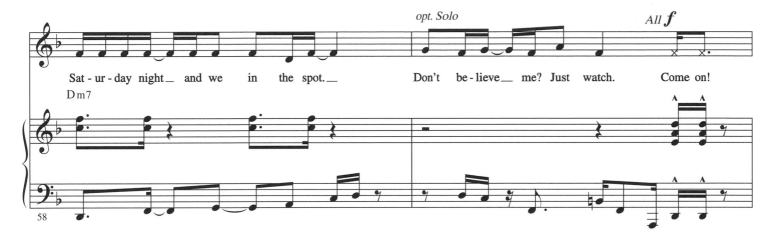

Don't be - lieve__ me? Just watch. Don't be - lieve__ me? Just watch. Don't be - lieve__ me? Just watch.__

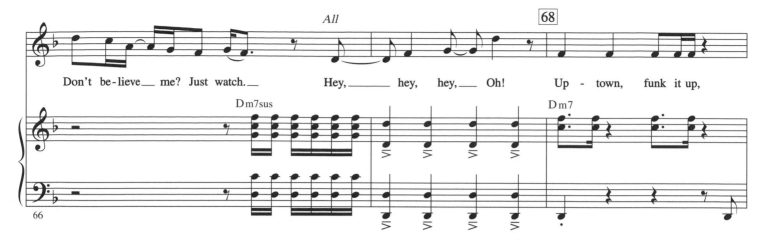

Don't be-lieve__ me? Just watch.__ Hey,__ hey, hey,__ Oh! Up - town, funk it up,

up - town, funk it up. Up - town, funk it up, up - town, funk it up.

Up - town, funk it up, up - town, funk it up. Up - town, funk it up,

up - town, funk it up. Come on! Up - town, funk it up!